Belief in prophethood is critical for every Muslim. In this book, we seek to clarify important questions related to this belief and instill a deep appreciation for all of the prophets of Allah (SWT).

To do so, we first reiterate the key principle that the prophets (upon them be peace) are, first and foremost, role models for all of mankind. This means that each and every human being has the potential to perfect their character and faith if they closely follow the prophets' etiquettes and examples. In this sense, the prophets are a direct link between Allah (SWT) and us.

But if Allah (SWT) has made them so perfect, how can prophets be role models for us? Here, it is important to state that although the prophets were the best humans, they were ultimately still *human beings*, like each of us. Remember that Allah (SWT) commands the Prophet Mohammed (SAW) to tell people: "I am merely a (mortal) man like you, but God has revealed to me that He is One!" (Qur'an 18:110). Recognizing the prophets' humanity gives us even more *himma* (motivation) to emulate them!

Finally, as Muslims we must also remember how important it is to love and honor *all* of Allah (SWT)'s beloved prophets. As the Holy Qur'an advises, righteous believers must "make no distinction between any of them, and to Allah do we surrender" (2:136).

In our first story, *The Peak of Perfection*, Amira and her friends discover the life and teachings of Prophet Jesus (AS), and realize that he is a role model for Muslims. In the second story, *Show Me the Way*, Asad learns the value of listening to a guide and relates this to following the sunnah of Prophet Mohammed (SAW), which will always lead us to the right path.

**Credits & Honors**

Creative Developers: Maryum Mohsin & Kenneth Molloy

Art Director: Annie Idris

Editors: Amin Aaser & Sana Aaser

Researcher: Armaan Siddiqi

**Glossary**

*As Salaam Alaikum – Peace be upon you*

*Alhumdulillah – All praise is for Allah*

*Bismillah – In the name of Allah*

*Winter break is only a week away. Ethan sits with the four friends at lunch.*

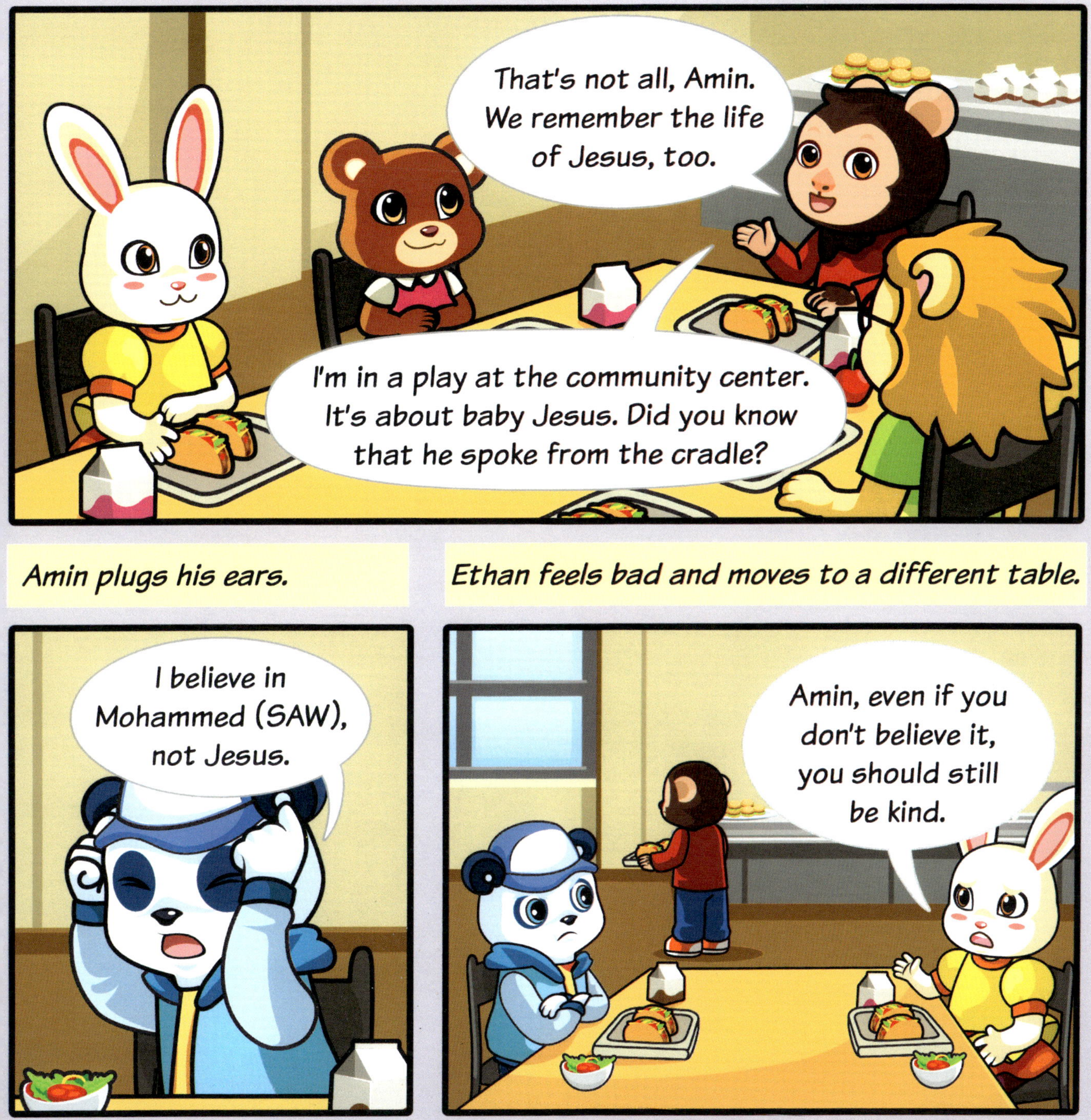

That's not all, Amin. We remember the life of Jesus, too.

I'm in a play at the community center. It's about baby Jesus. Did you know that he spoke from the cradle?

*Amin plugs his ears.*

*Ethan feels bad and moves to a different table.*

At home, Amira keeps thinking about what happened at lunch.

Amin is a good friend.

Ethan is a good friend, too.

Mom notices that Amira is sad.

Amira tells Mom what happened at school.

*Mom takes Amira to the Grove Art Museum.*

*Amira is happy to see so many beautiful pieces of art.*

*A painting of the Ark of Prophet Noah (AS)...*

*...a painting of the staff of Prophet Moses (AS)...*

*...and a painting of the mosque of Prophet Mohammed (SAW).*

*Shaykh Tahir joins Amira at a painting she is admiring.*

Of course, my dear! Abraham, Noah, David, Moses, Jesus, and our beloved Prophet Mohammed (SAW), we Muslims love them all!

**Questions :**

1. What does it mean to be a role model?
2. Can you be a role model? How?
3. Who are your role models? Why?

*Amira listens carefully. Shaykh Tahir continues.*

*The next day, Amira joins her friends at school.*

*Amin feels regretful for the way he treated Ethan.*

*The friends decide to make a video about Prophet Jesus (AS).*

*Over the next week, the friends...*

*...learn about Prophet Jesus (AS)...*

*...shoot a video on Asad's camera...*

*...and edit it for the internet.*

*Amin emails the video to Ethan.*

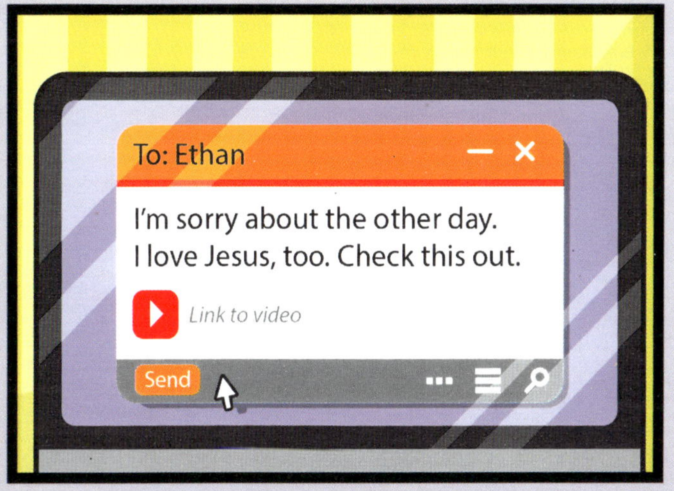


**Think About It**

Should Ethan forgive Amin?
View the video and decide!
NoorKids.com/Jesus

Discussion:
Prophets are our role models. Ask your parents how a story about one of our prophets has changed their lives.

# Prophets in the Qur'an

## Matching Activity

| | | |
|---|---|---|
| Harun (Aaron) |  | The son of Ibrahim and Hagar who has to be sacrificed. |
| Ismail (Ishmael) | 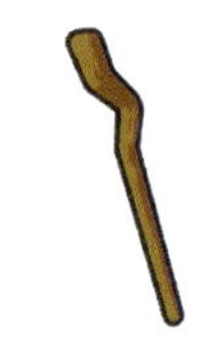 | He parted the Red Sea with his staff and crossed with the children of Israel. |
| Musa (Moses) |  | The first man. |
| Adam |  | The brother of Musa. |
| Ayyub (Job) |  | Swallowed by a whale. |
| Isa (Jesus) |  | This prophet had great patience. |
| Yunus (Jonah) |  | The son of Miriam (Mary) healed lepers and the blind. |

Ibrahim (Abraham)

He was a mighty king who knew the language of the birds and sent a letter to Bilqis, Queen of Saba.

Sulaiman (Solomon)

The last prophet sent by Allah (SWT) for all mankind.

Ya'qub (Jacob)

He slew the giant, Goliath. Father of Sulaiman.

Mohammed (SAW)

This prophet built the ark.

Yusuf (Joseph)

He was the father of all prophets who built the Kaaba with his son, Ismail.

Dawud (David)

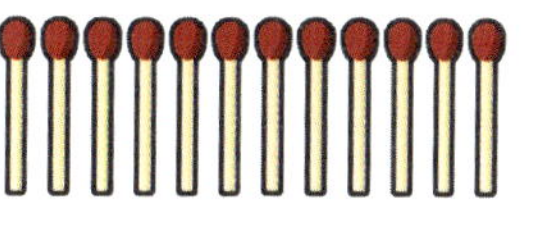

He had 12 sons, one of which was Yusuf.

Nuh (Noah)

This prophet was able to interpret dreams and was said to be very handsome.

*Asad and Mom are going to Mountain Fair.*

It means 'In the name of Allah.' Saying it before we do anything links our actions to the worship of Allah (SWT).

*Mom parks the car and the two walk toward the entrance.*

*Mom and Asad wait in line.*

Yes. Allah (SWT) has told us in the Holy Qur'an that the messenger of Allah is the best example for us. (33:21)

Prophet Mohammed (SAW) is our guide. If we do as he did, we will never be lost.

*Finally, they reach the front of the line.*

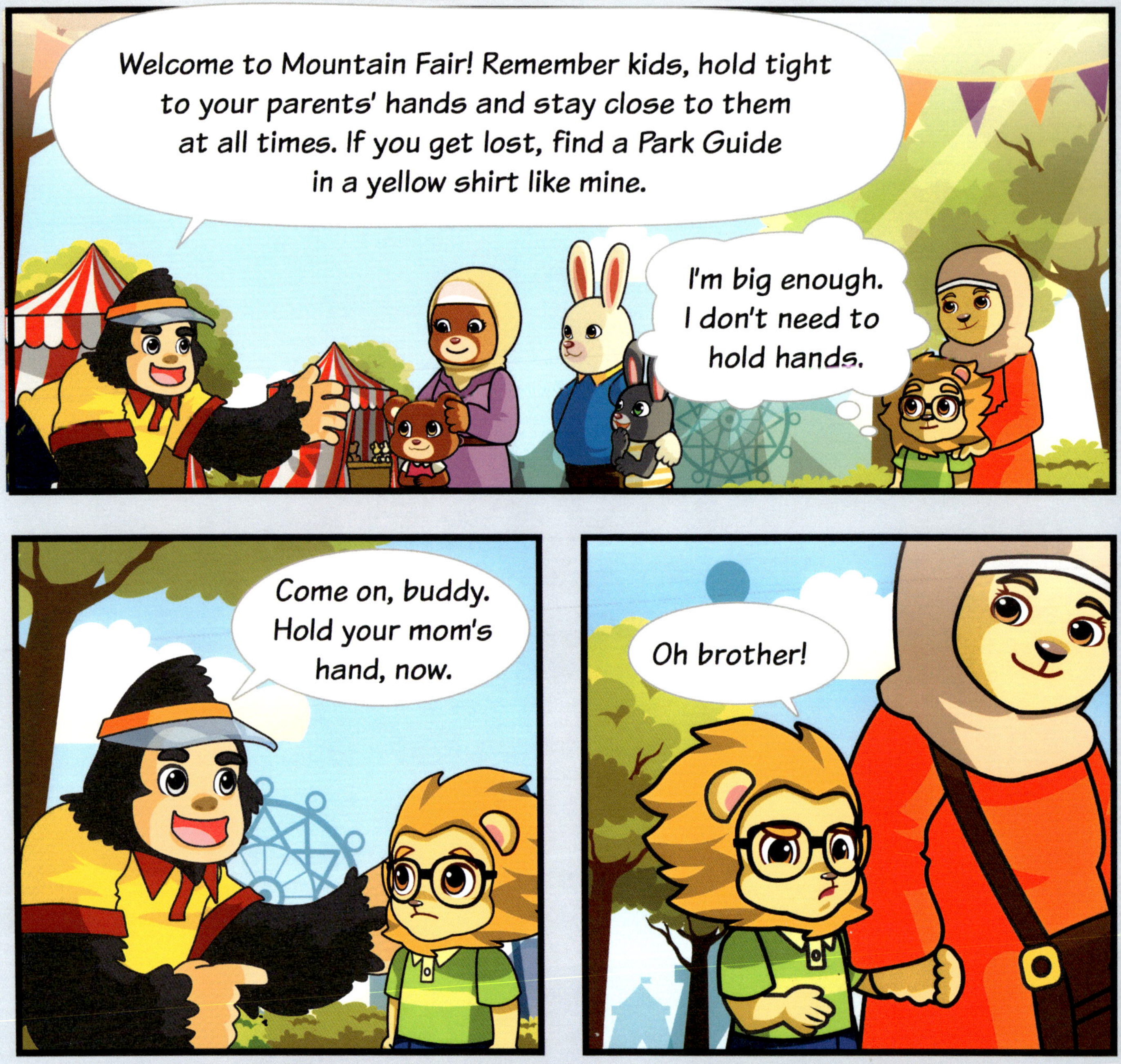

Welcome to Mountain Fair! Remember kids, hold tight to your parents' hands and stay close to them at all times. If you get lost, find a Park Guide in a yellow shirt like mine.

I'm big enough. I don't need to hold hands.

*Asad and Mom spend the entire day at Mountain Fair. They fly in the Super Summer Swings. They swirl in the Rapturous Rider.*

*They splash through The Surge.*

*Asad wants to see the Magic Show.*

*Mom gets a phone call.*

*Asad pushes his way to the side of the path.*

## Questions :

1. Have you ever been lost before?

2. What should Asad do?

*Asad arrives at the center of the park.*

*The Park Guide leads Asad down a side path.*

*At every turn, it seems the Park Guide knows just where to go.*

*Asad is reunited with Mom.*

I was so worried about you.

I'm sorry that I sneaked off. I wanted to see the Magic Show.

Wandering around lost, I missed out on a lot of fun that I could have been having with you.

## Questions :

1. How can listening to a guide help you?
2. Why is the Prophet (SAW) the best guide?
3. What are some ways you follow the sunnah of the Prophet (SAW)?

*Mom hugs Asad close.*

*Mom takes Asad to see the Magic Show.*

*Before they leave Mountain Fair, Mom buys an ice cream cone for Asad.*

# Islamic Inventions

## CAN YOU SPOT the 10 differences?

### Did You Know?

The dome is one of the main features of Islamic architecture. Domes are three-dimensional arches that draw your gaze up toward the heavens. They also light up the inside of buildings.

Muslim architects improved domes by adding squinches and ribs. This made the building process easier and created more complex design. Today, domes are seen in many places such as the Dome of the Rock in Jerusalem, Hagia Sophia in Istanbul, the Taj Mahal in Agra, and Masjid an-Nabawi (pictured above) in the holy city of Madinah.